Glendale Library, Arts & Culture Dept.

3 9 0 1 0 0 5 5 0 6 5 9 5 1

S0-DUW-076

NO LONGER PROPERTY OF
GLENDALE LIBRARY,
ARTS & CULTURE DEPT.

THE LOS ANGELES ANGELS OF ANAHEIM

BY
MARK STEWART

NORWOOD HOUSE PRESS

CHICAGO, ILLINOIS

j 796.3576 STE

Norwood House Press
P.O. Box 316598
Chicago, Illinois 60631

For information regarding Norwood House Press, please visit our website at:
www.norwoodhousepress.com or call 866-565-2900.

All photos courtesy of Getty Images except the following:
Topps, Inc. (6, 15, 20, 21, 23, 28, 31, 34 top, 45), SportsChrome (9, 10, 11, 35 top, 39),
Tom DiPace (14), Black Book Partners Archives (16, 17, 22, 35 bottom right, 37, 40, 42 bottom, 43 both),
Author's Collection (30, 33), Exhibit Supply Co. (36), SSPC (41),
Dell Publishing Co. (42 Top), Matt Richman (48).
Cover Photo: Stephen Dunn/Getty Image

The memorabilia and artifacts pictured in this book are presented for educational and informational purposes,
and come from the collection of the author.

Editor: Mike Kennedy
Designer: Ron Jaffe
Project Management: Black Book Partners, LLC.
Special thanks to Topps, Inc.

Library of Congress Cataloging-in-Publication Data

Stewart, Mark, 1960-
   The Los Angeles Angels of Anaheim / by Mark Stewart.
      p. cm. -- (Team spirit)
   Includes bibliographical references and index.
   Summary: "A Team Spirit Baseball edition featuring the Los Angeles Angels
of Anaheim that chronicles the history and accomplishments of the team.
Includes access to the Team Spirit website, which provides additional
information, updates and photos"--Provided by publisher.
   ISBN 978-1-59953-485-5 (library : alk. paper) -- ISBN 978-1-60357-365-8
(ebook) 1. Los Angeles Angels (Baseball team)--History--Juvenile
literature. I. Title.
   GV875.A6S74 2012
   796.357'640979496--dc23
                                            2011048175

© 2012 by Norwood House Press.
Team Spirit® is a registered trademark of Norwood House Press.
All rights reserved.
No part of this book may be reproduced without written permission from the publisher.
•••••
The Los Angeles Angels of Anaheim is a registered trademark of Angels Baseball LP.
This publication is not affiliated with The Angels,
Major League Baseball, or The Major League Baseball Players Association.

Manufactured in the United States of America in North Mankato, Minnesota.
196N—012012

COVER PHOTO: The Angels celebrate a good defensive play in 2011.

TABLE OF CONTENTS

ABOUT OUR GLOSSARY

In this book, there may be several words that you are reading for the first time. Some are sports words, some are new vocabulary words, and some are familiar words that are used in an unusual way. All of these words are defined on page 46. Throughout the book, sports words appear in **bold type**. Regular vocabulary words appear in ***bold italic type***.

MEET THE ANGELS

Part of the fun of playing baseball is getting your uniform dirty. The Los Angeles Angels of Anaheim know this better than anyone. After a game, their uniforms are full of dirt and grass stains, and even a rip or two. That's because the Angels play with the same passion they had as kids.

Talent and skill get a player to the **big leagues**. It takes effort and heart for a team to win. That is what the Angels are all about. Their fans love them for giving everything they've got.

This book tells the story of the Angels. Their part of the country is known for its warm weather and relaxed lifestyle. But playing the Angels is no vacation. When teams step on the field in Anaheim, they know it's time to get their uniforms dirty, too—because the Angels always play to win.

The Angels celebrate their 2002 championship. At times like these, the players seem more like happy kids than grown-ups.

GLORY DAYS

During the 1950s and 1960s, **Major League Baseball** moved west for the first time. In 1958, the Giants and Dodgers of the **National League (NL)** moved from New York to California. Three years later, the **American League (AL)** also added a new team in California, the Los Angeles Angels. They shared a ballpark with the Dodgers for four seasons.

LOS ANGELES ANGELS

In 1965, the team changed its name to the California Angels. A year later, they moved south to the city of Anaheim. During the 1960s, the Angels did a good job finding young talent. They amazed the experts when they finished third in the AL in 1962. Their leading hitters during this *decade* included Jim Fregosi, Buck Rodgers, Bobby Knoop, Jose Cardenal, Jay Johnstone, and Rick Reichardt. Among their top pitchers were Dean Chance, Jim McGlothlin, and Bob Lee.

In the years that followed, the Angels relied more and more on pitching. Andy Messersmith, Clyde Wright, Nolan Ryan, and Frank Tanana were all big winners in the 1970s. But the team needed better hitting before it could compete for a championship. To strengthen their offense, the Angels turned to **veterans** such as Rod Carew, Bobby Grich, and Don Baylor. They helped the team reach the top of the **AL West** in 1979.

The Angels won the AL West crown again in 1982. Their roster included several more experienced players, including Reggie Jackson,

LEFT: This trading card shows the 1961 Angels.   **ABOVE**: Fans mob the Angels after the team's AL West championship in 1982.

Bob Boone, Doug DeCinces, and Tommy John. In 1986, the Angels took the AL West for the third time. A young first baseman named Wally Joyner was the star of the club. That October, the Angels came within one out of reaching the **World Series**. Unfortunately, they suffered a heartbreaking loss to the Boston Red Sox.

Many years passed before the Angels and their fans recovered from this defeat. They had some good players in the 1990s, including Tim Salmon, Jim Edmonds, J.T. Snow, Chuck Finley, and Troy Percival. However, it was not until Mike Scioscia took over as manager of the Angels that they became *contenders* again.

In 2002, the team won the AL West for the first time in 16 seasons. Salmon and Percival were now the leaders of the club. They

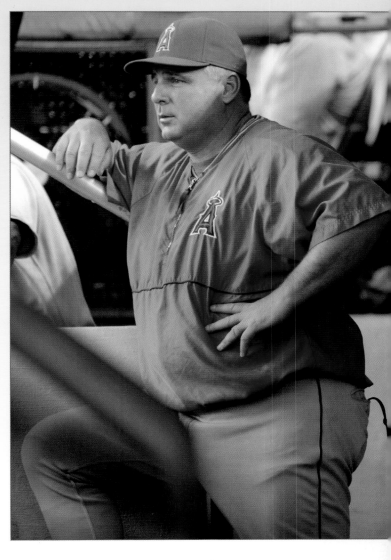

LEFT: Nolan Ryan won 138 games for the Angels in the 1970s.
ABOVE: Mike Scioscia watches the action from the dugout. He helped turn the Angels into one of baseball's best teams.

were joined by new stars, including Garret Anderson and Troy Glaus. Scioscia made sure everyone was ready to play at all times. Every victory seemed to produce a new hero. The Angels pitched well, played great defense, and never gave up. In the **playoffs**, the team played its best when the pressure was on. The Angels advanced to the World Series and celebrated their first championship with a victory over the San Francisco Giants.

Since then the team has finished first or second in the AL West almost every year. New faces replaced the old ones. In 2005, the team changed its name to the Los Angeles Angels of Anaheim.

ABOVE: Garret Anderson   **RIGHT**: Jered Weaver

The team kept fans coming to the ballpark by finding new players for the lineup. John Lackey, Chone Figgins, Francisco Rodriguez, Vladimir Guerrero, Torii Hunter, Ervin Santana, and Jered Weaver all joined the team from 2002 to 2008. In 2011, the Angels added two more stars, Albert Pujols and C.J. Wilson.

With their fans behind them, the Angels continued to win. They finished first in the AL West five times from 2004 to 2009. The Angels did not make it back to the World Series during those years, but

they put an excellent team on the field season after season. The players and fans knew it was only a matter of time before the Angels would be playing for a championship again.

HOME TURF

I n 1966, the Angels moved from the Los Angeles area to a new stadium in Anaheim, which is also home to Disneyland and other theme parks. The new ballpark was named Anaheim Stadium, but everyone called it the "Big A" after the gigantic A-frame scoreboard that rose more than 200 feet in the air. Today it is called Angel Stadium of Anaheim.

In 1998, the team's stadium was redesigned by Walt Disney Imagineering. The project cost $100 million. Angel Stadium is now a cozy, comfortable place to play and watch baseball. Whenever the Angels win, they light up a *halo* that rises high above one of the stadium's parking lots.

BY THE NUMBERS

- The Angels' stadium has 45,389 seats.
- The distance from home plate to the left field foul pole is 330 feet.
- The distance from home plate to the center field fence is 400 feet.
- The distance from home plate to the right field foul pole is 330 feet.

Fans bang together their inflatable "ThunderStix" to root for the Angels in their home park.

The Angels have used a lot of different letters on their caps and helmets over the years. In the 1960s, the team put *LA* on its hat when it started in Los Angeles. After they became the California Angels, the players wore caps with the letters *CA*. In the 1970s, the Angels used a lower case *a* and then switched to an upper case *A*—each with a halo around it. In the 1990s, the *CA* made a comeback.

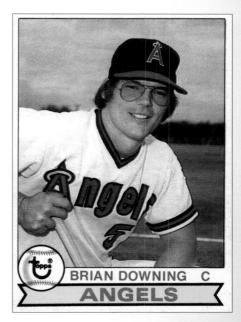

BRIAN DOWNING C
ANGELS

For most of the team's history, its main colors were dark red, deep blue, and white. However, when the Angels reached the World Series in 2002, their main uniform color was bright red. The letter on the team's cap was once again a big *A* with a halo around it. In 2011, the Angels introduced a special red jersey that celebrated their 50th anniversary.

LEFT: The *A* on Erick Aybar's 2011 cap and jersey is surrounded by the team's familiar halo. **ABOVE**: Brian Downing's 1970s uniform also features a halo around the letter *A*.

WE WON!

From 1961 to 2001, Angels fans spent each winter wondering, *What went wrong?* In 2002, they could not stop talking about everything that went right. The club reached its first World Series and won the championship with a thrilling comeback.

When the season started, no one even expected the Angels to make the playoffs. The team had finished 41 games behind the first-place Seattle Mariners in 2001. The 2002 Angels had the same players and the same manager, so the fans just crossed their fingers and hoped for the best.

In past years, the Angels' top players always seemed to get hurt. In 2002, everyone was healthy. The Angels won 99 games and made the playoffs as a **Wild Card**.

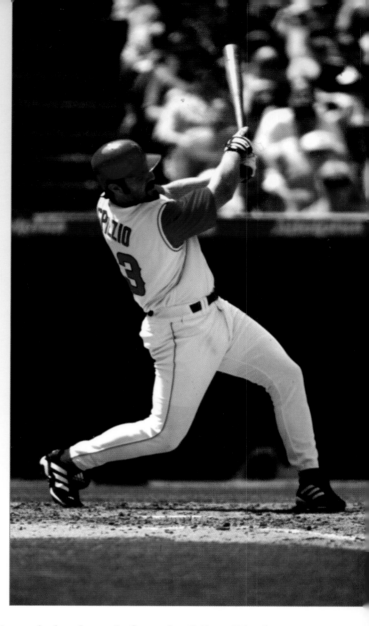

LEFT: Kevin Appier won 14 games in 2002.
RIGHT: Scott Spiezio hit better than .300 in the 2002 playoffs.

The Angels had a very balanced team. The offense was led by sluggers Troy Glaus, Garret Anderson, and Tim Salmon. They were supported by other good hitters such as Scott Spiezio, Darin Erstad, and Brad Fullmer. **Rookie** John Lackey joined Ramon Ortiz, Jarrod Washburn, and Kevin Appier in the **starting rotation**. The secret of the team's success was a great **bullpen**, which starred Francisco Rodriguez and Troy Percival.

To get to the World Series, the Angels had to defeat the New York Yankees and Minnesota Twins in the playoffs. Against New York, the Angels' hitters were on fire. They batted .376 as a team and won the series easily.

17

Against the Twins, the pitchers were the stars. They limited Minnesota to only seven runs in the first four games, and the Angels won three times to take a 3–1 lead in the series. Needing just one more victory to win the **pennant**, the Angels fell behind 5–3 in the fifth game, but they exploded for 10 runs in the seventh inning. Two innings later, they were AL champions for the first time.

In the World Series, the Angels faced the San Francisco Giants. Both teams had made the playoffs as Wild Cards, so it was hard to say which team would be better in a best-of-seven series. The Giants won Game 1, but the Angels won the next game 11–10. The teams split the next two games, and

ABOVE: Troy Glaus had several big hits during the 2002 World Series.
RIGHT: Garret Anderson delivers the game-winning double in Game 7.

the Giants won Game 5. San Francisco needed just one more victory to win the World Series.

Two nights later, Giants fans were getting ready to celebrate when their team led 5–0 in the seventh inning. The Angels scored three times to make the score 5–3. In the eighth inning, Glaus stepped to the plate with the bases loaded. He belted a long double to clear the bases and give the Angels a 6–5 victory. It was the most important hit in team history.

In Game 7, Anderson hit a double with the bases loaded to give the Angels a 4–1 lead. The bullpen kept the Giants from scoring any more runs, and the Angels were world champions!

GO-TO GUYS

To be a true star in baseball, you need more than a quick bat and a strong arm. You have to be a "go-to guy"—someone the manager wants on the pitcher's mound or in the batter's box when it matters most. Fans of the Angels have had a lot to cheer about over the years, including these great stars …

 THE PIONEERS

JIM FREGOSI   Shortstop

- BORN: 4/4/1942 • PLAYED FOR TEAM: 1961 TO 1971

Jim Fregosi was the best all-around player on the Angels during their first 10 years. Fregosi was a steady shortstop with a powerful bat. He was an **All-Star** six times and later was the manager of the Angels.

NOLAN RYAN   Pitcher

- BORN: 1/31/1947 • PLAYED FOR TEAM: 1972 TO 1979

Nolan Ryan threw harder than any pitcher in baseball. He was nicknamed the "Ryan Express." In 1973, Ryan pitched two **no-hitters** and set a new record for strikeouts with 383.

DON BAYLOR

Outfielder/Designated Hitter

• BORN: 6/28/1949 • PLAYED FOR TEAM: 1977 TO 1982

The first Angel to win a **Most Valuable Player (MVP)** award was Don Baylor. He led the league with 120 runs and 139 **runs batted in (RBIs)** in 1979, when the Angels won the AL West.

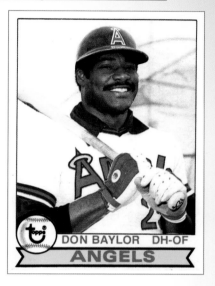

BOBBY GRICH

Second Baseman

• BORN: 1/15/1949 • PLAYED FOR TEAM: 1977 TO 1986

Bobby Grich was the league's best second baseman when he played for the Angels. He was an excellent fielder and a powerful hitter.

BRIAN DOWNING

Catcher/Outfielder

• BORN: 10/9/1950 • PLAYED FOR TEAM: 1978 TO 1990

When Brian Downing joined the team, he changed his **batting stance** and became one of the league's top hitters. Downing set many team batting records during his 13 seasons in Anaheim.

ROD CAREW

First Baseman

• BORN: 10/1/1945 • PLAYED FOR TEAM: 1979 TO 1985

The Angels traded for Rod Carew in 1979. He batted .318 that season and was named an All-Star. The Angels, meanwhile, made it to the playoffs for the first time.

LEFT: Jim Fregosi   **ABOVE**: Don Baylor

21

JIM ABBOTT   Pitcher

• BORN: 9/19/1967   • PLAYED FOR TEAM: 1989 TO 1992 & 1995 TO 1996

Jim Abbott went directly from college to the big leagues and won 40 games in his first three seasons with the Angels. Abbott was born without a right hand. He would deliver his pitch and quickly slip his left hand into his glove so he would be ready to field.

TIM SALMON   Outfielder

• BORN: 8/24/1968

• PLAYED FOR TEAM: 1992 TO 2006

Tim Salmon was the Angels' top slugger during the 1990s. He was voted the **Rookie of the Year** in 1993. Salmon was a player teammates respected and opponents feared.

GARRET ANDERSON   Outfielder

• BORN: 6/30/1972

• PLAYED FOR TEAM: 1994 TO 2008

Garret Anderson was a smart hitter who was at his best when a championship was on the line. In 2002, he drove in the winning runs in Game 7 of the World Series. In 2004, he got the hit that beat the Oakland A's for the AL West title.

TROY PERCIVAL   Pitcher

• BORN: 8/9/1969   • PLAYED FOR TEAM: 1995 TO 2004

Troy Percival had 30 or more **saves** eight times for the Angels. Even more amazing, he began his baseball career on the other side of home plate, as a catcher!

JERED WEAVER   Pitcher

• BORN: 10/4/1982   • FIRST YEAR WITH TEAM: 2006

Jered Weaver was a great pitcher in college who continued to win in the big leagues. He hid the ball so well before throwing it that hitters often couldn't see it until it was too late to swing. In 2010, he led the AL in strikeouts.

MARK TRUMBO   First Baseman

• BORN: 1/16/1986   • FIRST YEAR WITH TEAM: 2010

Mark Trumbo was supposed to be a fill-in while first baseman Kendry Morales recovered from an injury in 2011. Trumbo ended up leading all rookies in homers and RBIs. The Angels were so impressed that they voted him team MVP!

ALBERT PUJOLS   First Baseman

• BORN: 1/16/1980   • FIRST YEAR WITH TEAM: 2012

The Angels rarely miss a chance to improve their team. They proved this when they signed Albert Pujols after the 2011 season. Pujols was the league MVP three times with the St. Louis Cardinals.

LEFT: Tim Salmon   **RIGHT**: Mark Trumbo

For most of their first 50 years, the Angels were more famous for their owners than their managers. From the 1960s to the 1990s, Gene Autry ran the club. He was a famous "singing cowboy" in the movies. He used the money he made as a Hollywood star to buy the Angels. He cared deeply about the players and fans, and they loved him.

After Autry, the Walt Disney Company owned the Angels. The company put Bill Stoneman in charge of the team's business. Stoneman had pitched for the Angels in the 1970s and was a very smart judge of talent.

In 2000, Stoneman hired Mike Scioscia as the Angels' new manager. Scioscia was a catcher during his playing career. As a manager, he made sure his pitchers were focused and ready. He coached his hitters to be smart at the plate and do whatever was necessary to score a run. With Scioscia in the dugout, the Angels were usually able to win the close games.

In Scioscia's first 10 years, the team made it to the playoffs six times. No Angels manager had ever done that before. He was

Gene Autry shakes hands with Rod Carew. Autry signed Carew as a player in 1978. Carew stayed with the team as a batting coach after retiring in 1985.

named Manager of the Year in 2002 when the Angels won their first championship. Scioscia took home the award again in 2009.

The Angels' third owner, Arte Moreno, bought the team in 2004. He was one of 11 children who grew up in a two-bedroom house in Arizona. Moreno had great success in business. He relied on that experience to continue the Angels' winning *tradition*. Under Moreno, the team added many good players and signed Scioscia to a contract that would keep him in Anaheim for a long time.

There were a lot of teams better than the Angels in 1973, but none more exciting. Their star pitcher, Nolan Ryan, had an amazing year. He pitched a no-hitter against the Kansas City Royals in May and another no-hitter against the Detroit Tigers in July. Every time Ryan pitched, fans jammed the ballpark hoping to see him make history.

On September 27, the Angels faced the Minnesota Twins. Ryan was pitching in his last game of the year. He had a chance to break the record for strikeouts in a season. Ryan already had 367 strikeouts—15 short of the mark set by Sandy Koufax in 1965. Could Ryan strike out 16 Twins? That is what everyone had come to see.

The Minnesota batters were helpless against Ryan. In the eighth inning, he struck out Steve Brye to tie the record. Unfortunately, Ryan felt a sharp pain in his right thigh—he had torn a muscle. This meant he could not push off the **pitching rubber** and throw his

BALL STRIKE OUT BATTER AVG
.151

Nolan Ryan breathes a sigh of relief after his record-breaking 383rd strikeout.

hardest. With the score tied 4–4, Ryan decided to stay in the game. He did not strike out anyone in the ninth or 10th innings.

In the 11th inning, the Twins had a runner on second base with two outs. Ryan gritted his teeth, reared back, and fired three blazing fastballs past Rich Reese for his 383rd strikeout. The Angels scored in the bottom of the 11th to win 5–4. Ryan had his 21st victory of the season and was baseball's new strikeout king.

LEGEND HAS IT

HOW WERE THE ANGELS ABLE TO DRAFT SO MANY GOOD PLAYERS IN THEIR FIRST YEAR?

BOB RODGERS
Catcher

ANGELS

LEGEND HAS IT that they had "friends in high places." The people who built the Angels were extremely well liked around baseball, and they were especially close to the scouts for the Los Angeles Dodgers and San Francisco Giants. Their friends helped them identify many future stars they could pick from other teams, including Jim Fregosi, Dean Chance, Buck Rodgers, and Leon Wagner.

ABOVE: Bob "Buck" Rodgers
RIGHT: Jimmie Reese poses with the bat that made him famous.

OW GOOD WAS ANGELS COACH MIE REESE AT HITTING 'FUNGOES'?

LEGEND HAS IT that he was baseball's
all-time fungo king. Reese was a coach for the
Angels during the 1960s and 1970s. His job
was to hit fly balls during warm-ups with a long,
thin fungo bat. Reese was so accurate with this
bat that he could hit the flagpoles behind the
outfield fence. Once, during batting practice, he hit fungoes from
the pitcher's mound right across home plate to the Angels' hitters!

HO WAS THE ANGELS' BEST DANCER?

LEGEND HAS IT that Francisco Rodriguez was. Most
baseball fans knew Rodriguez as "K-Rod." He got the nickname
because he struck out so many batters. As a rookie in 2002,
Rodriguez helped the Angels win the World Series. In 2008, he
set a record with 62 saves. Long before Rodriguez reached the
big leagues, he used another talent to help support his family.
In his boyhood home in Venezuela, Rodriguez was known as
"Nene Fran," which is Spanish for Baby Fran. To earn money,
he would put on break-dancing shows to Michael Jackson music.

n 1964, baseball scouts were all talking about the same player His name was Rick Reichardt, and the power-hitting outfielde was one of the top stars in college baseball. Reichardt was also one of the best players in college football. That meant there would be a lot of competition to sign him after he graduated.

The Angels believed that Reichardt would make them contender in the American League. Back then, there was no **draft** in baseball Teams often got into contests to see which club could offer the most money to a young **prospect**. Wealthy teams such as the Angel had a big advantage. Their owner, Gene Autry, had made millions in the movie business. Whatever other teams were willing to pay Reichardt, Autry simply offered more.

Finally, Reichardt agreed to join the Angels. He was given a bonus of $200,000—by far the bigges amount ever paid to an **amateur** baseball player a the time. Reichardt did well for the Angels for a couple of seasons, but he never became a superstar. At one point

LEFT: Gene Autry was willing to spend whatever it took to build a winning team.   **RIGHT**: Rick Reichardt chose baseball over football, and the Angels paid the price.

Reichardt fell ill and had to have one of his kidneys removed.

Meanwhile, many people in baseball complained that the Angels had been irresponsible in signing Reichardt. Some team owners feared that the bonuses would keep going higher and higher. The teams with the most money would have a great advantage when it came to buying talent. If that happened, the rich clubs could pile up young stars at every position. That would be bad for baseball, because poorer teams might not be able to compete.

As a result, baseball changed the way it did business. In 1965, the owners voted to start a player draft. Each year, teams would take turns selecting the top players from high school and college. Today, the draft makes sure that each team gets an equal chance to sign the best amateur players.

TEAM SPIRIT

W hen Angels fans cheer their loudest, the team gets an extra burst of energy. The players love it when the fans make the ballpark shake. There have been times, in fact, when all the screaming and stomping was actually the difference between winning and losing.

Unfortunately, cheering fans aren't always enough. That means it's time for the Angels' famous rally monkey to start doing its thing on the stadium scoreboard. Fans call the monkey "Rally," though her name is actually Katie. She is a white-haired capuchin monkey. Rally bounces up and down to the song "Jump Around." The Angels made the monkey a star during the 2002 World Series. Now fans collect "autographed" pictures of Rally.

LEFT: Darin Erstad leads the Angels as they cheer for their home fans during the 2002 playoffs.   **ABOVE**: Rally "signed" this souvenir photo.

TIMELINE

Nolan Ryan

1961
The Angels play their first season.

1965
The team changes its name to California Angels.

1973
Nolan Ryan throws two no-hitters.

1962
The Angels finish third in just their second year in the league.

1966
The Angels move to a new stadium in Anaheim.

1979
Don Baylor wins the MVP and leads the team to its first AL West title.

Anaheim Stadium was nicknamed the "Big A" for its A-shaped scoreboard.

Torii Hunter batted .299 for the 2009 team.

1982
The Angels win the AL West for the second time.

2007
Francisco Rodriguez is the winning pitcher in the **All-Star Game**.

2009
The Angels win the AL West for the third year in a row.

2002
The Angels win the World Series.

2004
Vladimir Guerrero wins the MVP.

2011
Jered Weaver is the starting pitcher in the All-Star Game.

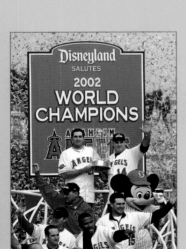

The Angels celebrate their victory in the 2002 World Series.

Vladimir Guerrero

Fun Facts

STREAKY

Jered Weaver tied a league record by starting his career with nine victories in a row. He had another hot streak in 2011. Weaver was 6–0 on April 25. No pitcher had ever won six games that quickly to start a season.

DOH!

Mike Scioscia is one of the only athletes to appear on two different episodes of *The Simpsons*. He played himself in 1992 and again in 2010.

A LITTLE GOES A LONG WAY

Angels outfielder Albie Pearson was the shortest man in baseball at 5′ 5″. That did not stop him from leading the league with 115 runs scored in 1962.

ABOVE: Albie Pearson
RIGHT: Ervin Santana

FAMOUS FIRST

In 1983, Fred Lynn hit the first **grand slam** in the history of the All-Star Game.

GETTING EVEN

In his first six seasons, Ervin Santana had never won a game against the Cleveland Indians. He took care of that when he faced them in July of 2011. Santana struck out 10 batters and pitched a no-hitter.

WALLY WORLD

In 1986, rookie Wally Joyner was the starting first baseman for the AL in the All-Star Game. It was the first time baseball fans had ever voted a first-year player onto the team.

BIG JOHN

In 2002, John Lackey became the first rookie in 93 years to start and win the seventh game of a World Series.

TALKING BASEBALL

"In the movies, I never lost a fight. In baseball, I hardly ever won one."

▶ **GENE AUTRY**, ON THE CHALLENGES OF OWNING A BASEBALL TEAM

"What's important is how you're playing, not who you're playing or where you're playing."

▶ **MIKE SCIOSCIA**, ON HOW WINNING TEAMS LOOK AT EACH GAME

"Hitting is an art, but not an exact science."

▶ **ROD CAREW**, WHO BATTED .328 FOR HIS CAREER

"I wanted to be like Nolan Ryan."

▶ **JIM ABBOTT**, ON THE PLAYER HE IDOLIZED AS A KID

"I love to hit that little round ball out of the park and make them say, 'Wow!'"

▶ **REGGIE JACKSON**, ON HITTING LONG HOME RUNS

"I get paid a lot of money to play a game with the greatest players in the world. What could be better than that?"

▶ **JIM EDMONDS**, ON THE THRILL OF PLAYING IN THE MAJORS

"It took every single guy out there to win this."

▶ **TROY PERCIVAL**, ON THE ANGELS' 2002 CHAMPIONSHIP

LEFT: Jim Abbott
RIGHT: Troy Percival

GREAT DEBATES

People who root for the Angels love to compare their favorite moments, teams, and players. Some debates have been going on for years! How would you settle these classic baseball arguments?

JIM FREGOSI WAS THE BEST SHORTSTOP IN ANGELS HISTORY ...

... because he was an excellent hitter, a great fielder, and one of the smartest players the team ever had. Fregosi was an All-Star six times from 1964 to 1970. He helped set a new standard for shortstops. During his playing days, very few shortstops were good hitters. Fregosi made fans look at the position differently. He finished among the Top 10 in batting average twice, in hits four times, and in triples seven years in a row.

YOU SURE ABOUT THAT? DAVID ECKSTEIN GETS THE EDGE OVER FREGOSI ...

... because he helped the Angels win a championship. Eckstein (**LEFT**) did not have as much talent as Fregosi, but he always found a way to help his team win. In 2002, Eckstein batted .293 and scored 107 runs. That season he also led the AL in **sacrifice bunts** and in getting hit by a pitch. There is just no way the Angels would have won the World Series without him.

... because it helped the Angels reach the playoffs in 1979 and 1982. The team sent four players to the Minnesota Twins for Carew, including a good outfielder named Ken Landreaux. Carew batted over .300 in his first five years with the Angels and was an All-Star six times. He also got his 3,000th hit as a member of the Angels.

NO WAY! TRADING JIM FREGOSI TO THE NEW YORK METS WAS AN EVEN BETTER MOVE ...

... because the Angels received Nolan Ryan (RIGHT) and three other players in the deal. Fregosi had already played 11 wonderful seasons for the Angels, but he was wearing out. Ryan was just coming into his own. He won 138 games in eight seasons with the Angels and led the AL in strikeouts six times. Ryan eventually made it into the **Hall of Fame**.

41

The great Angels teams and players have left their marks on the record books. These are the "best of the best" …

ANGELS AWARD WINNERS

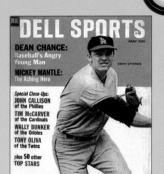

Dean Chance

Garret Anderson

WINNER	AWARD	YEAR
Leon Wagner	All-Star Game MVP	1962
Bill Rigney	Manager of the Year	1962
Dean Chance	Cy Young Award*	1964
Clyde Wright	Comeback Player of the Year	1970
Don Baylor	Most Valuable Player	1979
Fred Lynn	All-Star Game MVP	1983
John Candelaria	Comeback Player of the Year	1986
Bert Blyleven	Comeback Player of the Year	1989
Dave Winfield	Comeback Player of the Year	1990
Tim Salmon	Rookie of the Year	1993
Tim Salmon	Comeback Player of the Year	2002
Mike Scioscia	Manager of the Year	2002
Troy Glaus	World Series MVP	2002
Garret Anderson	All-Star Game MVP	2003
Vladimir Guerrero	Most Valuable Player	2004
Bartolo Colon	Cy Young Award	2005
Mike Scioscia	Manager of the Year	2009

The annual award given to each league's best pitcher.

ANGELS ACHIEVEMENTS

ACHIEVEMENT	YEAR
AL West Champions	1979
AL West Champions	1982
AL West Champions	1986
AL Pennant Winners	2002
World Series Champions	2002
AL West Champions	2004
AL West Champions	2005
AL West Champions	2007
AL West Champions	2008
AL West Champions	2009

ABOVE: Chone Figgins led the 2005 team with 186 hits.
LEFT: Gene Mauch, Bob Boone, and Doug DeCinces meet on the mound during a 1982 game.

PINPOINTS

T he history of a baseball team is made up of many smaller stories. These stories take place all over the map—not just in the city a team calls "home." Match the pushpins on these maps to the **TEAM FACTS**, and you will begin to see the story of the Angels unfold!

1 Los Angeles, California—*The team played here from 1961 to 1965.*

2 Anaheim, California—*The team has played here since 1966.*

3 San Francisco, California—*The Angels played in the 2002 World Series here.*

4 Minneapolis, Minnesota—*The Angels played for the 2002 AL pennant here.*

Wally Joyner

5 Refugio, Texas—*Nolan Ryan was born here.*

6 Tucson, Arizona—*Arte Moreno was born here.*

7 Wooster, Ohio—*Dean Chance was born here.*

8 Chicago, Illinois—*Leon Wagner was named the 1962 All-Star Game MVP here.*

9 Flint, Michigan—*Jim Abbott was born here.*

10 Atlanta, Georgia—*Wally Joyner was born here.*

11 Nizao Bani, Dominican Republic—*Vladimir Guerrero was born here.*

12 Caracas, Venezuela—*Francisco Rodriguez was born here.*

GLOSSARY

🧠 BASEBALL WORDS
🧠 VOCABULARY WORDS

AL WEST—A group of American League teams that play in the western part of the country.

ALL-STAR—A player who is selected to play in baseball's annual All-Star Game.

ALL-STAR GAME—Baseball's annual game featuring the best players from the AL and NL.

AMATEUR—Someone who plays a sport without being paid.

AMERICAN LEAGUE (AL)—One of baseball's two major leagues; the AL began play in 1901.

BATTING STANCE—The way a hitter stands at home plate.

BIG LEAGUES—The top level of professional baseball.

BULLPEN—The area where a team's relief pitchers warm up. This word also describes the group of relief pitchers in this area.

CONTENDERS—People who compete for a championship.

DECADE—A period of 10 years; also specific periods, such as the 1950s.

DRAFT—The annual meeting at which teams take turns choosing the best players in high school and college.

GRAND SLAM—A home run with the bases loaded.

HALL OF FAME—The museum in Cooperstown, New York, where baseball's greatest players are honored.

HALO—A circle of light.

MAJOR LEAGUE BASEBALL—The top level of professional baseball. The AL and NL make up today's major leagues.

MOST VALUABLE PLAYER (MVP)—The award given each year to each league's top player; an MVP is also selected for the World Series and the All-Star Game.

NATIONAL LEAGUE (NL)—The older of the two major leagues; the NL began play in 1876.

NO-HITTERS—Games in which a team does not get a hit.

PENNANT—A league championship. The term comes from the triangular flag awarded to each season's champion, beginning in the 1870s.

PITCHING RUBBER—The rectangular slab on the pitcher's mound that marks the spot where pitchers must begin their wind-up.

PLAYOFFS—The games played after the regular season to determine which teams will advance to the World Series.

PROSPECT—A young athlete who is expected to become a star.

ROOKIE—A player in his first season.

ROOKIE OF THE YEAR—The annual award given to each league's best first-year player.

RUNS BATTED IN (RBIs)—A statistic that counts the number of runners a batter drives home.

SACRIFICE BUNTS—Bunts intended to advance a runner to his next base.

SAVES—A statistic that counts the number of times a relief pitcher finishes off a close victory for his team.

STARTING ROTATION—The group of pitchers who take turns beginning games for their team.

TRADITION—A belief or custom that is handed down from generation to generation.

VETERANS—Players with great experience.

WILD CARD—A playoff spot reserved for a team that does not win its division, but finishes with a good record.

WORLD SERIES—The world championship series played between the AL and NL pennant winners.

EXTRA INNINGS

TEAM SPIRIT introduces a great way to stay up to date with your team! Visit our **EXTRA INNINGS** link and get connected to the latest and greatest updates. **EXTRA INNINGS** serves as a young reader's ticket to an exclusive web page—with more stories, fun facts, team records, and photos of the Angels. Content is updated during and after each season. The **EXTRA INNINGS** feature also enables readers to send comments and letters to the author! Log onto:

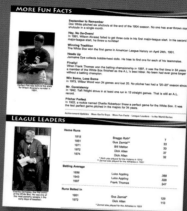

www.norwoodhousepress.com/library.aspx

and click on the tab: **TEAM SPIRIT** to access **EXTRA INNINGS**.

Read all the books in the series to learn more about professional sports. For a complete listing of the baseball, basketball, football, and hockey teams in the **TEAM SPIRIT** series, visit our website at:

www.norwoodhousepress.com/library.aspx

ON THE ROAD

LOS ANGELES ANGELS OF ANAHEIM
2000 Gene Autry Way
Anaheim, California 92806
(714) 940-2000
losangeles.angels.mlb.com

**NATIONAL BASEBALL
HALL OF FAME AND MUSEUM**
25 Main Street
Cooperstown, New York 13326
(888) 425-5633
www.baseballhalloffame.org

ON THE BOOKSHELF

To learn more about the sport of baseball, look for these books at your library or bookstore:

- Augustyn, Adam (editor). *The Britannica Guide to Baseball*. New York, NY: Rosen Publishing, 2011.

- Dreier, David. *Baseball: How It Works*. North Mankato, MN: Capstone Press, 2010.

- Stewart, Mark. *Ultimate 10: Baseball*. New York, NY: Gareth Stevens Publishing, 2009.

INDEX

ABOUT THE AUTHOR

MARK STEWART has written more than 50 books on baseball and over 150 sports books for kids. He grew up in New York City during the 1960s rooting for the Yankees and Mets, and was lucky enough to meet players from both teams. Mark comes from a family of writers. His grandfather was Sunday Editor of *The New York Times,* and his mother was Articles Editor of *Ladies' Home Journal* and *McCall's.* Mark has profiled hundreds of athletes over the past 25 years. He has also written several books about his native New York and New Jersey, his home today. Mark is a graduate of Duke University, with a degree in history. He lives and works in a home overlooking Sandy Hook, New Jersey. You can contact Mark through the Norwood House Press website.